i

U.S. NONPROLIFERATION POLICY TOWARDS NORTH KOREA

The United States policy for dealing with a nuclear North Korea has been a combination of containment, deterrence, and limited engagement since the enactment of the 1994 Agreed Framework. While this and earlier policies have prevented war on the Korean peninsula, such approaches have not prevented North Korea from developing a nuclear program and proliferating this technology, as well as missile technology, to numerous countries not friendly to the United States. In order to stop North Korea from transferring weapons technology, the United States needs a new strategic concept. This paper will examine four options that may be used to support the element of the U.S. National Security Strategy of preventing the proliferation of nuclear weapons.

Recently, North Korea has committed two belligerent acts upon South Korea. First was the sinking of the South Korea warship *Cheonan* on 26 March 2010 in which 46 sailors from the South died. The North is suspected of sinking the ship, but has not taken responsibility. On 23 November 2010, North Korea shelled the South Korean island of Yeonpyeong with approximately 200 rounds of artillery, killing two South Korean marines and two South Korea civilians. While these horrific actions are in violation of the 1953 armistice agreement ending the Korean War, the main concern of the United States regarding North Korea is its nuclear weapons program and the proliferation of weapons technology. The current U.S. National Security Strategy (NSS) states that "there is no greater threat to the American people than weapons of mass destruction, particularly the danger posed by the pursuit of nuclear weapons by violent extremists and their proliferation to additional states."[1] In regards to North Korea, the

NSS discusses engaging the North with the end state being "the denuclearization of the Korean peninsula."[2] The strategy further states, "If North Korea eliminates its nuclear weapons program...they will be able to proceed on a path to greater political and economic integration with the international community. If they ignore their international obligations, we will pursue multiple means to increase their isolation and bring them into compliance with the international nonproliferation norms."[3] The U.S. policy of containment, deterrence, and limited engagement has not been successful. Dan Blumenthal states the United States needs a new policy based upon four realities. First, "North Korea already is a nuclear power and will not be talked into ceasing to be one."[4] Second, "The United States and its allies have very few sticks to use aside from military action–which is why engagement with North Korea has failed and will continue to fail."[5] Third, "The current lack of coherence and complicity in the fiction that North Korea can still be prevented from becoming a nuclear power is harming America's leadership position in Asia."[6] And fourth, "Military options either to remove nuclear weapons or remove the regime are too costly."[7] Before options are addressed to deal with North Korea, background information will be provided to frame the issue.

North Korea's Motives

Since North Korea is a closed society, it is at times difficult to determine the motives for their actions. In his book, *Red Rogue*, Bruce E. Bechtol, Jr. sums up the North's endstate the best. "North Korea has one overriding goal that trumps all others– regime survival."[8] To keep the regime in power, the North sees nuclear weapons as the key element in deterring the United States from a potential attack and regime change. They view their program as a crucial component in persuading the U.S. and other countries to have diplomatic dialogue to gain aid and other concessions. This is part of the North's overall strategy. Wade L. Huntley states that "North Korea's provocative actions probably flow from a calculated strategy of brinkmanship and coercive diplomacy. This strategy anticipates positive effects beyond the short-term rise in tension and animosity such actions elicit and has brought success in the past."[9] When one drills down into this strategy, there is a key element: North Korea's desire to be on the same level of prestige as the United States. *Jane's Sentinel Security Assessment – China and Northeast Asia* shows that "North Korea's key priority in its foreign policy has long been its relations with the U.S. and, in particular, the establishment of a peace treaty between Washington and Pyongyang."[10] There are three reasons why the North desires these relations with the United States. First, the North sees the United States as its main threat and a peace treaty would provide them with security. Second, the North wants to be treated in a similar manner diplomatically with South Korea. Third, the recognition of the North by the United States may allow them access to the World Bank and International Monetary Fund to assist in helping their struggling economy.[11] This means additional sanctions and diplomatic talks of the past will not change the North's behavior as they view the penalties for their actions as weak.[12]

North Korea's Belligerent Acts

North Korea has committed several belligerent acts over the last two decades. In addition to several missile tests, the North conducted two underground nuclear tests, one on October 9, 2006 and one on May 25, 2009. These tests are not the only acts of defiance North Korea has shown. Due to United Nations sanctions, the North has had to resort to other activities to support the regime's survival. Bruce Bechtol confirms that, "The evidence now shows that Pyongyang's illegal activities include not only money counterfeiting and weapons proliferation but highly lucrative heroin and

3

methamphetamine drug trade"[13] This evidence shows that North Korea is using ways and means to supplement its need for currency due to United Nations sanctions. What needs to be stressed here is the North's weapons proliferation; a vital interest to the United States. Bechtol points out that, "Most experts on North Korea and on national security policy agree that there are two primary threats from North Korea missiles: the threat to U.S. forces and their allies in Northeast Asia and the threat of proliferation throughout the Middle East and South Asia."[14] Pyongyang has increasingly engaged in weapons sales, included extended nuclear technology exchange programs, since 9/11, with countries such as Egypt, Iran, Libya, Pakistan, Syria, Vietnam, and Yemen.[15] North Korea also supported efforts in Syria to build a nuclear reactor that was of the exact same design as the reactor at Yongbyon, the North's known nuclear facility.[16] This technology, as Wade L. Huntley points out, shows that "North Korea's reinvigorated nuclear program gives it the potential to fuel proliferation by exporting fissile materials, nuclear weapons development technologies and expertise, or even complete operational weapons."[17] This capability, as addressed in the ICG Asia Report Number 61, is "the single greatest threat posed by the DPRK is its export of fissile material or nuclear bombs to other countries or terrorist groups around the world."[18]

U.S. Responses to North Korea's Belligerent Acts

The United States has been content on allowing North Korea's bad behavior and has tried since 1994 to engage Pyongyang, occasionally through dialogue, to no avail. The United States did try to negotiate an agreement with Pyongyang in 1994 to stop the North's nuclear program. The Agreed Framework was the first ever agreement between the United States and North Korea. However, this agreement fell apart. Michael Breen, author of the book *Kim Jong-Il: North Korea's Dear Leader*, writes that in

4

1994, "Under the Agreed Framework, as it was called, the North froze its nuclear program and the U.S. created an international body called the Korean Energy Developmental Organization (KEDO) to build two light-water reactors and supply 500,000 tons of oil a year for free until construction was complete."[19] Breen further states that "In October 2002, the deal ruptured after Pyongyang was found pursuing a secret uranium-enrichment program. The U.S. halted the oil shipments and Pyongyang retaliated by expelling the international monitors who had been assigned to watch the spent fuel rods as part of the Agreed Framework, withdrawing from the Nuclear Nonproliferation Treaty."[20] The problem with the U.S. strategy is that it presents no "red lines" to North Korea. The North has no fear of U.S. retaliation because America has been weak on the issue.   Since 2002, North Korea has been left unchecked on their nuclear program. The problem with U.S. policy can be seen twofold by Stephen Blank. First, "The policy of having no red lines and thresholds for truly unacceptable behavior illustrates with great starkness just how much of U.S. policy was ultimately nothing more than a bluff."[21] Second, "Seen from Seoul and Beijing, if not Moscow, American policy, focused on terminating the DPRK's program, and too often arguing for regime change thus appears to be threatening or leading to a war not nonproliferation."[22]

The question is if current U.S. policy has prevented North Korea from developing a nuclear program and exporting its technology to other countries. The answer is no. Even though one of North Korea's demands is to be removed from the list of state sponsored of terrorism, the North has not complied by following policies that would lead to that removal. Gregory J. Moore states that "the United States did not prevent North Korea from acquiring and testing nuclear weapons, despite its deterrent strategies, its diplomatic efforts, its ultimatums, and U.S.-sponsored UN Security Council resolutions against it."[23] There are signs that the North should comply with the non-proliferation treaty. Gregory L. Schulte writes that, "Since the first atomic bomb was assembled, 18 countries have chosen to dismantle their nuclear weapons programs. Countries such as Argentina, Libya, South Africa, and Switzerland made this decision for a variety reasons, but foremost among them was the desire to improve their international standing. Another important factor was foreign pressure, especially from the United States."[24] However, since the 1994 Agreed Framework, North Korea has not complied with any agreements they have made. Hence, the six-party talks are an example of failed American diplomacy.

Six-Party Talks

The six-party talks were an attempt to bring North Korea and the interested parties in the nuclear debate, China, South Korea, Japan, Russia, and the United States to the negotiating table to resolve the North's nuclear issue. These talks, which began in 2003 and have ended so far in 2008, have produced no results. Jane's Sentinel Security Assessment portrays the best overview of the six-party talks. "Six rounds of the six-party talks subsequently took place, all of which were held in Beijing. The first three (August 2003, February 2004 and June 2004) were followed by a 13-month hiatus as a result of fundamental disagreement between the two main protagonists, the United States and North Korea. The fourth and longest round of talks so far began at the end of July 2005 and ended in early September, before yet another suspension of the process as a result of U.S. sanctions and the North Korea nuclear test in October 2006. The reinvigorated six-party format restarted in December 2006 as the second phase of the fifth round. The six-party talks stalled in the second phase of the sixth round, which officially ended in September 2007. In early October 2008, North Korea agreed to continue disablement of its Yongbyon facility and allow verification of a June 2008 declaration of its nuclear activities in return for the delisting from the U.S. Department of State's list of states sponsoring terrorism. However, the second-phase actions of the negotiations (verification and disablement) were not completed. The last meeting between six-party delegation heads took place in December 2008."[25] The six-party talks have been a failure for a variety of reasons; including the motivations of the other parties in the talks and the fact that North Korea could not be talked into eliminating its nuclear program. The talks have also allowed the North to continue its weapons program without any consequences. Finally, the talks are not the forum the North Koreans wants to deal from; they want to deal diplomatically with the United States on a unilateral level.

United Nations Resolutions and Sanctions

There have been three United Nations Security Council Resolutions as a result of North Korea's two nuclear tests and missile launches. Even though these resolutions were passed with China's approval, they have had little effect on North Korea's behavior. The North has found ways to absorb the pain of sanctions through illegal activities, even though the impact on its populous has been severe. The North views sanctions as short-term pain to their ultimate goal of dealing with the United States on a one-on-one basis. The United Nations resolutions have had little to no effect on North Korea and continued sanctions will not work due to the North's elicit activities, especially its nuclear program. Stephan Haggard and Marcus Nolan make two points regarding sanctions against North Korea. First, "those countries most inclined to sanction North

Korea do not trade with or invest in it; they have even seen economic relations decline."[26] Second, "given the extreme priority that the regime places on its military capacity, it is unlikely that the pain the world can bring to bear will induce North Korea to surrender its nuclear weapons."[27] Finally, sanctions will never work on North Korea unless China assists in the enforcement of such actions. China has made clear that they will not enforce the inspection and enforcement of North Korean shipping in accordance with the United Nations resolutions.

China

China has been a proponent and host of the six-party talks for one reason: it is in their interest to keep the status quo on the Korean peninsula. Between 50%-75% of North Korea's trade is with China.[28] Even though China has condemned North Korea's nuclear test, which could destabilize the region if South Korea or Japan decide to go nuclear, China has other motives. The first is explained by Wade L. Huntley. "China's interests in North Korea are broader than the nuclear issue. China experienced a massive refugee influx during North Korea's famine in the mid-1990s and thus is particularly sensitive to its neighbor's wider economic and political stability. From Beijing perspective, a collapse of the governance there would mean certain chaos on its border and a host of uncertainties as to outcomes."[29] In addition, China fears that the collapse of North Korea may mean the United States could be next to its border. Stephan Blank addresses four key points to China's strategy on North Korea. First, "China will neither sacrifice North Korea to America nor insist on it total denuclearization despite Pyongyang's exasperation of China."[30] Second, "the fear that U.S. policy might lead to either war or a collapse of the DPRK has galvanized China to seize the

8

diplomatic initiative in unprecedented ways that have clearly strengthened its overall position in Asia and improved its relation with South Korea."[31] Third, "Although North Korea's non-nuclearization is a vital priority for China, preserving peace and stability on the peninsula outranks it. Indeed, China probab y has a greater stake in preserving North Korea's stability than do any of the other players. …China's stake in North Korean survival is demographical (refugees being a major fear), economic, and strategic."[32] Finally, the "American view concerning China's leverage upon the DPRK actually underestimates the increasingly discernible mutual dislike that underlies the allegedly fraternal relationship."[33] One can deduce from this data that China wants a stable North Korea and one that is favorable to its national interests and objectives.[34]

<u>South Korea</u>

South Korea is the most interested player in the issues with North Korea. Even though they were not a signatory to the 1953 armistice agreement, they have had to deal with most of the belligerent acts of the North. Having spent five years stationed in the South, the author can confirm that the South does not want war with the North, and even wants a co-existence with the hermit state of the North. The South has built the greater Seoul metropolitan area within a few mi es of the border with the North, within easy distance of the North's artillery. The South's strategic thinking can be summed up by Jong-Yun Bea, "the South has preferred coexistence, collaboration, and cooperation with North Korea rather than to compete with it."[35] Finally, like China, South Korea is concerned with the possibility of refugees in the event of collapse of the North Korean regime or armed conflict.

Option #1: Continue the Current Policy of Containment/Deterrence

The United States has dealt with North Korea over the past 50-plus years with a policy of containment and deterrence. This policy has been successful in the fact it has prevented an invasion of South Korea. Gary S. Kinne sums up the hallmarks of our current containment policy: "A strategy of containment (ways) has maintained a relative peace on the Korean peninsula for the later part of the twentieth century. The resources (means) committed to execute this strategy include a strong military presence for deterrence; near diplomatic isolation; enactment of economic trade sanctions and embargoes; and a sustained anti-North Korean information campaign."[36] However, this policy has not prevented North Korea from developing a nuclear weapons program and has not stopped weapons proliferation. In his article *Coming to Terms with Containing North Korea*, David E. Sanger states, "The problem is that every American president since Harry Truman has underestimated how much rot the North Korean regime could withstand. Each thought the North could fall on his watch. After all, it has been the most sanctioned nation on earth since the early 1950's, and it has recently cut the few deep economic ties that it made in the past decade with the South."[37] Sanger also makes a point that one should not compare the U.S. strategy towards North Korea with that of the Soviet Union: "there are reasons to wonder whether containment of North Korea can work. The core idea is that wariness and time are the best instruments with which to let a corrupt, inept government rot from within, as when the Soviet Union collapsed."[38] In addition, the world has changed over the past 50 years. Kinne points out in his assessment of North Korea that "the new global environment demands that we reevaluate our current policy of containment. Despite containment's past effectiveness, North Korea has opted to revitalize it WMD production capability and proliferation efforts. No longer does the strategy of containment, specifically diplomatic isolation of the North, seem a viable option in itself."[39]

While some argue the U.S. containment and deterrence policy has failed, others view the policy as the only option to deal with North Korea. Bruce E. Bechtol, Jr. argues that "only deterrence has kept North Korea from threatening the South, attempting to bully other nations in the region with WMD (such as Japan), and using its government to violate international laws."[40] While this is a true statement, the proliferation of weapons technology from North Korea has not ceased. Blumentha is a proponent of a containment strategy that would have three objectives: "(1) continuing to protect South Korea from attack; (2) deterring a nuclear or conventional attack on the U.S. homeland or on its allies and friends; and (3) preventing the proliferation of North Korea of WMD to rogue regimes and terrorist organizations."[41] Again, the main question with these objectives is stopping the proliferation issue. Without the support of the international community, especially China, to interdict shipments of nuclear and weapons material, the United States is limited in its ability to stop the proliferation of these items. In addition, since North Korea views the interdiction of its shipping as an act of war, the United States has shown refrain from conducting such operations.[42]

Option #2: U.S. Military Withdrawal

The withdrawal of U.S. military forces from the Korean peninsula is predicated on several assumptions. These include the South Korean military is capable of defending itself; the North Korean military is not the formidable force it once was; and China, Japan, and South Korea can deal with the North Korean issue on their own. This option may also be favored in South Korea, especially the younger generation, as they see the presence of U.S. forces in their country an invasion of their national sovereignty. There

11

are several key facts that support the withdrawal of U.S. forces from the peninsula. The first is the capability of the North Korean military. David E. Sanger states "that North Korea no longer instills fear the way it did even during the Clinton presidency, when it threatened to turn Seoul into a "sea of fire" if it did not get its way."[43] He further argues that the North Koreans do not have enough fuel to keep their air force in the air very long and the "South Koreans are so unafraid of a 1950s-style invasion that they have built housing developments to the edge of the demilitarized zone dividing the Koreas."[44] Doug Bandow affirms the lack of capability within the North Korean military, stating, "The North's military equips under-trained, malnourished soldiers with ancient equipment. One American aircraft carrier has more firepower than the entire North Korean military. What of Pyongyang's putative nuclear arsenal? The North probably hasn't miniaturized any weapons that it might have constructed. North Korea also doesn't have a missile capable of hitting America, let alone doing so accurately."[45] Bandow further argues that even though South Korea is threatened by the North, the threat is not that great. "The Republic of Korea is far ahead on most measures of national power. The South's forces are better trained and its equipment is more capable; Seoul has a much larger army reserve and military industrial base. South Korea has twice the population and upwards of 40 times the GDP of the North."[46] Based upon military capability alone, U.S. forces are not required to defend South Korea. In addition, when one looks at a map of Asia, it is North Korea's neighbors, China, Japan, and South Korea, that should have an issue with the North's behavior, not the United States.[47] Also, since North Korea has not honored any deal that has been negotiated with them, the United States might be well served by leaving this problem to the country's most effected in the region.[48]

While there is an argument to withdrawal U.S. forces from the Korean peninsula, there are also reasons to keep these forces forward deployed. First of all, the U.S. presence in South Korea shows Washington's commitment to the region and our allies.[49] These forces are also able to respond to other hotspots within Asia if required.[50] In addition, while the South Korean military is better trained and equipped than North Korea, they still lack the aviation and reconnaissance/surveillance capabilities that U.S. forces currently provide. The withdrawal of U.S. forces would also take a considerable amount of time and cost both South Korea and the United States a large amount a funding.[51] Most importantly however, is whether China, Japan, and South Korea cannot control North Korea, in particular, the proliferation of weapons technology. The ICG Asia Report Number 61 shows that "if key regional countries did not dissuade or otherwise prevent a nuclear-armed North Korea, then the demonstration effect of allowing the North to 'get away with it' would further encourage would-be proliferators."[52] The report further states that North Korea could become "the world's leading supplier of nuclear technology, fissile material or nuclear bombs to other 'rogue' states or terrorist organizations like al Qaeda. If this occurred, the international security environment would deteriorate severely."[53]

Option #3: Military Action Against North Korea

A military attack against North Korea with surgical strikes to take out their nuclear sites or change the regime is an option, but there are many disadvantages to such action. There are however, proponents of an all out invasion of North Korea. Retired general's Thomas McInerney and Paul Vallely state that "our combined forces (South

Korea and the United States) could defeat North Korea decisively in thirty to sixty days. There is no doubt on the outcome. If North Korea refuses to end its nuclear program—and if China refuses to force North Korea to end it—we need to make it clear that we will act decisively to take out North Korea's weapons and its noxious regime."[54] This option suggests the only way to totally eliminate North Korea's nuclear weapons program is to defeat its military, occupy the country, and inspect the entire country.[55] Gregory J. Moore rightfully argues that such an attack has other issues, "at the same time it is not feasible to take out North Korea's nuclear capabilities with military strikes (even if the U.S. military could be certain where they all are) because of the likelihood that Seoul, a city of 14 million just 30 miles from the North Korean border, would be reduced to rubble by conventional North Korean artillery and missiles."[56] This highlights the main disadvantage to military strikes against North Korea: How will they react? Besides the threat of the North's artillery on Seoul, there is a potential they could use either chemical or biological weapons against South Korea, Japan, and U.S. forces in the area. There is also a risk fracturing the alliance the United States has with South Korea and Japan if such attacks took place. Would China enter the conflict supporting North Korea? Finally, and most importantly, the risk of military operations against North Korea may cost lives of hundreds of thousands of South Korea military personnel and civilians, produce thousands of American casualties, and cost of billions of dollars.

Option #4: A New Type of Engagement

As previous shown, the United States has attempted to engage North Korea through the Agreed Framework and the six-party talks. These forms of engagement have not prevented North Korea from developing a nuclear program and proliferating

14

weapons technology and material. For now, the United States must accept the fact that North Korea has a nuclear program that the North will not give up. John Feffer argues that U.S. policy makers are not approaching the North Korea issue adequately. "They see engagement as a reward for North Korea's good behavior. We will work on a peace treaty to replace the current Korean War armistice *if* North Korea returns to denuclearization. We will remove obstacles that stand between North Korea and engagement with the international community *if* North Korea shows signs of economic reform. We will pursue diplomatic relations *if* North Korea improves its human rights accord."[57] He argues that instead of continuing with confrontational engagement which has been the norm, the United States should seek constructive engagement. Charles Freeman states that "constructive engagement allows common interests to be pursued with another state, even as sharp differences continue to exist with it on some issues. The central element of constructive engagement is the conduct of diplomatic dialogue on matters of common strategic concern."[58]

The United States should constructively engage North Korea bilaterally. This type of engagement would cost the United States little and would potentially gain the support of North Korea's neighbors, especially China. Constructive engagement would include signing a peace treaty with North Korea and China to replace the existing Korean War armistice, which would officially end the Korean War. In addition, Washington should give North Korea full diplomatic recognition, something the North has asked for that would guarantee their security. This would give the North Korean leadership a pathway for a secure future. After diplomatic ties have been made, embassies could be opened in Washington and Pyongyang. The United States closest ally, the United Kingdom, has an embassy in North Korea already.[59] The key to this engagement is the United States needs to make the first move.[60] Gregory J. Moore lays out the advantages of such a strategy. If North Korea was agreeable to the United States' offer, there are two courses of action that may follow. The first course of action is that following the signing of a peace treaty and the opening of a United States embassy in North Korea, Pyongyang may feel the threat from the United States has subsided and be willing to surrender its' nuclear weapons program. The second course of action is if North Korea accepted the United States' offer and did not live up to the terms of the agreement, the United States would still have an advantage as they would have the capability to eavesdrop on the regime. These United States overtures to North Korea would be seen favorably to China, Russia, and South Korea. This is strategically important if sanctions were required against North Korea in the future.[61] There is a risk with this option that is addressed in the ICG Asia Report, "there is the risk the DPRK may not negotiate in good faith, but prefer to drag out negotiations. Buying time would allow Pyongyang to increase its nuclear capabilities—both it plutonium and HEU programs—thereby strengthening its hand either for a future negotiation or military confrontation."[62]

Reunification?

An often dismissed subject is the potential reunification of the Korean peninsula. Both South and North Korea have publicly stated their desires to be one country again, but this may only be rhetoric. There are only two ways in which the Koreas could be united: war or the collapse of North Korea. The military option has been addressed earlier and has enormous costs associated with it. The collapse of North Korea would also have enormous costs. In fact, the South Korea president, Lee Myung-bak, proposed a reunification tax, which was swiftly nixed. The issue of North Korea potentially collapsing is not improbable. Fareed Zakaria, in his article *When North Korea Falls*, makes a case that the collapse of North Korea could happen based upon information the North Korean populous is receiving. The North Koreans are not totally oblivious to what is going on outside their country. Cellular phone subscriptions number over 200,000 and South Korean DVDs are available on the black market. With this information, the North Koreans may understand that life in South Korea is better than in the North and social unrest certainly would occur. There may be a point where the North Koreans, with a gross national product of $1,900 versus the South's $28,100, start migrating south to better opportunities.[63] The problems with a potential North Korean collapse are several. First and foremost, who will pay the bill? North Korea's infrastructure will need billions of dollars to mirror that of the South. China and South Korea also do not want the North to collapse for fear of the millions of refugees that would destabilize not only both countries, but the global economic system as well. Finally, if the North collapsed and was eventually unified with the South, who would a unified Korea ally themselves with; the United States or China? It is in the best interests of all parties that the United States takes steps to constructively engage North Korea to avoid all hell breaking loose.[64]

A Way Ahead

The United States should engage North Korea bilaterally by signing a peace treaty and normalizing relations. This strategic concept is feasible, acceptable, and suitable in dealing with the North Korean nuclear issue. However, containment and deterrence should continue until a diplomatic agreement is in place and working in the interests of the United States. This option of constructive engagement would also be seen in a positive light with China, Russia, and South Korea.[65] This is important if North Korea decides to back out of any diplomatic agreements with the United States and continues to develop and proliferate weapons technology; it would be easier to apply sanctions or take other action if these countries see the North as not accepting such a deal.[66]

Recent events as a result of the North Korean shelling of Yeonpyeong indicate Pyongyang is ready to return to the negotiating table. China, and to a lesser extent North Korea, want to resume the failed six-party talks, which is nothing more than kicking the can down the road some more and giving the North more time to further develop its' nuclear weapons program. This is not in the best interests of the United States. The adoption of a new strategy is required as all others have failed to stop North Korea's proliferation of nuclear technology and material.

Endnotes

[1]Barack H. Obama, *National Security Strategy* (Washington, DC: The White House, May 2010), 4.

[2] Ibid., 23.

[3] Ibid., 23-24.

[4] Dan Blumenthal, *Facing a Nuclear North Korea*, AEI Online, July 8, 2005, http://www.aei.org (accessed October 18, 2010).

[5] Ibid.

[6] Ibid.

[7] Ibid.

[8] Bruce E. Bechtol, Jr., *Red Rogue: The Persistent Challenge of North Korea* (Dulles, VA: Potomac Books, 2007), 205.

[9] Wade L. Huntley, "U.S. Policy Toward North Korea in Strategic Context," *Asian Survey*, Volume 47, Issue 3, (2007), 476.

[10] "External Affairs, Korea, North – Relations with the US," *Jane's Sentinel Security Assessment – China and Northeast Asia*, April 15, 2010 (accessed October 27, 2010).

[11] Ibid.

[12] Gregory L. Schulte, "Stopping Proliferation Before it Starts," *Foreign Affairs*, Volume 89, Issue 4 (July/August 2010): in ProQuest (accessed October 27, 2010).

[13] Bechtol, *Red Rogue: The Persistent Challenge of North Korea,* 24.

[14] Ibid., 46.

[15] Ibid., 46.

[16] Schulte, "Stopping Proliferation Before it Starts."

[17] Huntley, "U.S. Policy Toward North Korea in Strategic Context."

[18] ICG Asia Report Number 61, "North Korea: A Phased Negotiation Strategy," (Washington/Brussels, August 1, 2003), 30.

[19] Michael Breen, *Kim Jong-Il: North Korea's Dear Leader* (Singapore: John Wiley &Sons, 2004), 38.

[20] Ibid.

[21] Stephen Blank, "The End of the Six-Party Talks?" *Strategic Insights*. Volume VI, Issue 1 (January 2007).

[22] Ibid.

[23] Gregory J. Moore, "America's Failed North Korea Nuclear Policy: A New Approach," *Asian Perspective*, Volume 32, Issue 4 (2008): in ProQuest (accessed October 27, 2010).

[24] Schulte, "Stopping Proliferation Before it Starts."

[25] "External Affairs, Korea, North – Relations with the US," *Jane's Sentinel Security Assessment – China and Northeast Asia*, April 15, 2010 (accessed October 27, 2010).

[26] Stephan Haggard and Marcus Nolan, "Sanctioning North Korea: The Political Economy of Denuclearization and Proliferation," *Asian Survey*, Volume 50, Number 3, 564.

[27] Ibid., 567.

[28] Mary Beth Nilitin et al., "North Korea's Second Nuclear Test: Implications of U.N. Security Council Resolution 1874," *Congressional Research Service* (July 1, 2009).

[29] Huntley, "U.S. Policy Toward North Korea in Strategic Context."

[30] Blank, "The End of the Six-Party Talks?"

[31] Ibid.

[32] Ibid.

[33] Ibid.

[34] Ren Xiao, "Korea's New Administration and Challenges for China's Relations with the Korean Peninsula," *Asian Perspectives*, Volume 32, Issue 2 (2008): in ProQuest (accessed October 27, 2010).

[35] Jong-Yun Bae, "South Korean Strategic Thinking Towards North Korea," *Asian Survey*, Volume 50, Number 2, 345.

[36] Gary S. Kinne, *U.S. Strategy Towards North Korea*, Strategic Research Project (Carlisle Barracks, PA: U.S. Army War College, May 3, 2004), 1.

[37] David E. Sanger, *Coming to Terms with Containing North Korea*, The New York Times, August 9, 2010, http://www.nytimes.com/2009/08/09/weekinreview/09sanger.html (accessed October 18, 2010).

[38] Ibid.

[39] Kinne, *U.S. Strategy Towards North Korea*, 4.

[40] Bechtol, *Red Rogue: The Persistent Challenge of North Korea*, 205.

[41] Blumenthal, *Facing a Nuclear North Korea*.

[42] Peter Crail, "UN Tightens North Korea Sanctions," *Arms Control Today*, Volume 39, Issue 6 (July/August 2009), in ProQuest (accessed October 27, 2010).

[43] Sanger, *Coming to Terms with Containing North Korea*.

[44] Ibid.

[45] Doug Bandow, *Time to Let the Neighbors Deal with the North Korean Problem*, Japan Times, October 17, 2010, http://ebird.osd.mil/ebfiles/e20101017782033.html (accessed October 18, 2010).

[46] Ibid.

[47] Ibid.

[48] ICG Asia Report Number 61, "North Korea: A Phased Negotiation Strategy," (Washington/Brussels, August 1, 2003), 22.

[49] Kinne, *U.S. Strategy Towards North Korea*, 6.

[50] Ibid.

[51] Ibid.

[52] ICG Asia Report Number 61, "North Korea: A Phased Negotiation Strategy," 22.

[53] Ibid.

[54] Thomas McInerney and Paul Vallely, *Endgame: The Blueprint for Victory in the War on Terror* (Washington, DC: Regnery Publishing, 2004), 80.

[55] ICG Asia Report Number 61, "North Korea: A Phased Negotiation Strategy," 28.

[56] Moore, "America's Failed North Korea Nuclear Policy: A New Approach."

[57] John Feffer, *North Korea: Why Engagement Now?* Institute for Policy Studies, August 13, 2010, http://www.ips-dc.org/articles/north_korea_why-engagement_now (accessed October 18, 2010.

[58] Charles Freeman, *Arts of Power: Statecraft and Diplomacy* (Washington, DC: U.S. Institute of Peace Press, 1997), 80-81.

[59] Moore, "America's Failed North Korea Nuclear Policy: A New Approach."

[60] Ibid.

[61] Ibid.

[62] ICG Asia Report Number 61, "North Korea: A Phased Negotiation Strategy," 25.

[63] Fareed Zakaria, *When North Korea Falls...*, Washington Post, October 18, 2010, http://ebird.osd.mil/ebfiles/e20101018782165.html (access October 18, 2010).

[64] Moore, "America's Failed North Korea Nuclear Policy: A New Approach."

[65] Ibid.

[66] Ibid.